Trumpet I in B♭

BRASS ON BROADWAY

arranged for brass quintet
by Bob Lowden

intermediate level

THE CANADIAN
BRASS

C A N A D I A N
B R A S S
**SERIES OF
COLLECTED QUINTETS**

BROADWAY BABY
(From *FOLLIES*)

1st TRUMPET

Words and Music by
Stephen Sondheim

COMEDY TONIGHT
From *A FUNNY THING HAPPENED ON THE WAY TO THE FORUM*

1st TRUMPET

Words and Music by
Stephen Sondheim

GET ME TO THE CHURCH ON TIME

(From *My Fair Lady*)

1st TRUMPET

Words by Alan Jay Lerner
Music by Frederick Loewe

OL' MAN RIVER
(From *SHOW BOAT*)

1st TRUMPET

Words by Oscar Hammerstein II
Music by Jerome Kern

SUNRISE, SUNSET
(From *FIDDLER ON THE ROOF*)

1st TRUMPET

Words by Sheldon Harnick
Music by Jerry Bock

CANADIAN BRASS
SERIES OF COLLECTED QUINTETS

BRASS ON BROADWAY

arranged for brass quintet
by Bob Lowden

contents

Welcome to the *Canadian Brass Series of Collected Quintets*. In our work with students, for some time we have been aware of the need for more brass quintet music at easy and intermediate levels of difficulty. We are continually observing a kind of "Renaissance" in brass music, not only in audience responses to our quintet, but to all brass music in general. The brass quintet, as a chamber ensemble, seems to have become as standard a chamber combination as a string quartet. That could not have been said twenty-five years ago. Brass quintets are popping up everywhere — professional quintets, junior and senior high school ensembles, college and university groups, and amateur quintets of adult players.

We have carefully chosen the literature for these collected quintets, and closely supervised the arrangements. Our aim was to retain a Canadian Brass flavor to each arrangement, and create attractive repertory designed so that any brass quintet can play it with satisfying results. We've often remarked to one another that we certainly wish that we'd had quintet arrangements like these when we were students!

Happy playing to you and your quintet.

— THE CANADIAN BRASS

ISBN-13: 978-1-4584-0166-3
Distributed By

50488778

U.S. $8.99

HL50488778

7777 W. BLUEMOUND RD. P.O. BOX 13819 MILWAUKEE, WI 53213